D1515356

VARMINT HUNTING

JUDY MONROE PETERSON

rosen publishing's
rosen central

New York

To Dave, thank you from my heart

Published in 2011 by The Rosen Publishing Group, Inc.
29 East 21st Street, New York, NY 10010

Library of Congress Cataloging-in-Publication Data

Peterson, Judy Monroe.
Varmint hunting / Judy Monroe Peterson. — 1st ed.
    p. cm. — (Hunting: pursuing wild game!)
Includes bibliographical references and index.
ISBN 978-1-4488-1245-5 (library binding) —
ISBN 978-1-4488-2275-1 (pbk.) —
ISBN 978-1-4488-2276-8 (6-pack)
1. Varmint hunting—Juvenile literature. I. Title.
SK336.P48 2011
799.2'5—dc22

2010015514

Manufactured in Malaysia

CPSIA Compliance Information: Batch #W11YA: For further information, contact Rosen Publishing, New York, New York, at 1-800-237-9932.

On the cover: A raccoon is considered a varmint, or pest. Young raccoons spend their first months living in tree holes.

CONTENTS

*H*unting animals called varmints is a form of pest control. Small mammals that are considered varmints include raccoons, opossums, coyotes, bobcats, and prairie dogs. Nuisance animals eat or damage property, including livestock or pets. They may eat farm crops. Varmint hunting is a wildlife management tool used as a way to control nuisance animal populations. Hunting controls excess animal populations, providing farmers and ranchers with a valuable method of restricting or eliminating nuisance wildlife populations so that they don't overrun and overgraze farmlands.

Varmint hunters may hunt to protect their property or livestock. In addition, they may help other people protect their property from varmints. An example is when coyotes kill and eat costly farm and ranch animals such as calves and lambs. Coyotes also catch and kill pet dogs and cats. On rare occasions, they may attack small children. Another example of varmint devastation is the damage that is caused by prairie dogs. These plentiful, energetic, and burrowing animals dig many deep holes in cropland or pastures. If cattle or horses step into the holes, they could break their legs. These injuries can result in costly veterinarian care or

North American coyotes are very effective predators that eat any bird or small animal. This coyote has caught a bobwhite quail, a popular game bird.

the death of the animals. Losing these valuable animals hurts the livelihood of farmers and ranchers.

Varmint hunting provides a unique opportunity for hunters to practice and improve their shooting skills year-round. Many varmints, such as coyotes, can be hunted during every month of the year. It is critical to know the laws that define what a varmint is, what license is required, and the time of year and time of day that hunting can take place. Varmint hunters must study, understand, and know the laws that apply to them. Varmint hunting regulations differ for each state. People can learn these regulations wherever they purchase hunting licenses.

The hunting of some varmints is not a sport usually attempted by beginners. Coyote and prairie dog hunters need special and expensive equipment, such as high-powered scopes and rifles. Some varmint hunters travel long distances to get to an animal's habitat. For instance, many hunters of prairie dogs must travel to the western United States to find the animals. Unlike small game hunting, hunters seldom find and shoot varmints in their backyard or in a hunting area that is close to their home. However, beginning hunters can find experienced varmint hunters who often will introduce them to the sport and share their equipment in a group hunt.

Varmint hunters find many reasons to enjoy their sport. Successful varmint hunters may be allowed to hunt small or big game on that landowner's property in exchange for varmint control. Varmint hunting provides a year-round shooting sport for hunters to refine their skills. Hunters like to pursue varmints because they are challenging to hunt. They are cautious and elusive animals and are often hunted at night. Some hunters sell their raccoon, coyote, and bobcat furs. Although people enjoy eating raccoon and opossum, such is not the case with coyotes, bobcats, and prairie dogs. Many varmint hunters report that they feel great satisfaction when they help rid farms and ranches of these nuisance animals.

CHAPTER 1

THE HUNT BEGINS

A wild animal that is called a varmint has many definitions, and these vary by state and geographical area. It is critical that hunters read, study, understand, and follow the local laws regulating the harvest of each type of varmint. The term "varmint" is seldom used within wildlife and hunting laws. Some states refer to them as nuisance animals. Hunters are responsible for knowing exactly what varmint animal can be hunted and when and how it can be hunted.

Why Some Animals Are Considered Varmints

Varmints are generally small game that are considered a nuisance or pest because of their overpopulation or their negative impact on people. The excess population

Prairie dogs can multiply quickly and destroy croplands or livestock fields with their numerous large burrows. These rodents live close together and easily transfer fleas and viruses to each other.

makes these small game animals a problem for people, particularly farmers and ranchers. In the United States, animals that are often considered varmints include raccoons, opossums, coyotes, bobcats, and prairie dogs.

Raccoons and opossums can destroy crops and damage property. Coyotes and bobcats can injure or kill valuable farm animals and pets. People and pets, such as dogs and cats, can die from rabies. This disease can be transmitted by the bite of an infected raccoon, opossum, or coyote. Prairie dogs are a significant reservoir of plague for other wildlife and pet animals. Plague is an infection transmitted by the bite of an infected flea. Prairie dogs can harbor infected fleas. To transmit the disease, the flea must bite a person. The plague can be cured in its early stages if treated by medications known as antibiotics. Without treatment, the plague is usually deadly. Prairie dogs can overpopulate a ranch or farm and cause damage to livestock and crops.

Varmint Hunting Regulations

No legal definition of a varmint exists in the United States. Each state determines which big or small wild animals are considered varmints. The definition of a varmint can change from state to state. The states' departments of natural resources publish the current hunting regulations on their Web sites and in free booklets. Sometimes varmints are open game on private land for year-round hunting in one state, but may have a controlled hunting season in an adjoining state. In addition, hunting regulations for varmints sometimes vary within areas of a state, such as the northern part of a state and its southern part.

State governments allow liberal hunting seasons and generous or unlimited bag limits for animals that, from time to time, are considered pesky varmints. The hunting of varmints is a management tool used by the states' departments of natural resources to control excess or nuisance wild animal populations. In many states, varmints are both hunted and trapped. Sometimes a state's regulations specify that people can hunt or trap a defined number of particular varmints per season.

Some states classify small game, such as raccoons, coyotes, and bobcats, as furbearing animals. During the hunting season, some states allow furbearers to be trapped. Whether hunted or trapped, this classification of varmint as a furbearer has a maximum per-season bag limit regardless of the method of animal harvest.

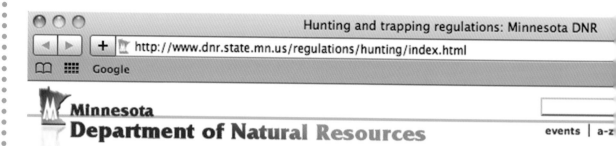

Hunting and trapping regulations: Minnesota DNR

http://www.dnr.state.mn.us/regulations/hunting/index.html

Google

Minnesota
Department of Natural Resources

events | a-z

Recreation | Destinations | Nature | Education / safety | Licens

Home > RLP > Regulations >

Regulations

- **Boating**
- Hunting
- **Fishing**
- **Off-highway vehicle**
- **Snowmobile**
- **Special Regulations**

Hunting & trapping

- **Main page**
- **Seasons**
- Regulations
- **Licenses**
- **Hunter education & safety training**
- **Hunter Recruitment & Retention**
- **Licensed shooting preserves** PDF
- Shooting ranges

Hunting and trapping regulations

2009 hunting regulations

Download the:

- **Minnesota Hunting and Trapping Regulations Handbook** PDF (4.5 MB)
  The online version of the 2009 Hunting and Trapping Regulations Handbook contains the latest corrections to the printed version. Corrected text is **highlighted in blue**, with the nearby margin marked using one of two update arrows shown below

  - **Camp Ripley Archery Hunt 2** - p. 93
  - **Coyote, striped skunk & other unprotected** - p. 43
- **2009 Firearms Deer Zone Map** PDF (3 MB)
- **2009 Waterfowl Hunting Regulations** PDF (2
  - **Spring Light Goose hunting regulation**

All states publish regulations and maintain Web pages (such as this one for Minnesota, http://www.dnr.state.mn.us/regulations/hunting/index.html) that define and update varmint hunting rules.

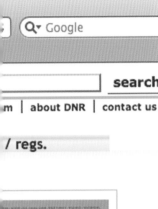

Raccoons and Opossums

Raccoons are widely considered to be a varmint. They can cause serious damage to farmland and livestock. Two favorite foods of raccoons are corn and eggs. Farmers who grow corn or raise poultry, such as chickens, turkeys, ducks, or geese, may find that raccoons are a serious threat to their livelihood. Many states have generous hunting seasons for this animal, from summer or fall through winter. The bag limit varies depending on the state and season. In Arkansas, for example, the bag limit is two per day in the fall, and there is no bag limit from mid-November through the end of March.

Opossums are a troublesome animal for farmers. They are a nuisance because they may live in and under farm buildings and destroy crops. Like raccoons, they will eat the eggs of a farmer's poultry. Farmers who have a large number of opossums on their property are usually willing to have hunters eliminate their varmint population. Many states have liberal hunting seasons for this animal. For example, in Wisconsin, no season limits, bag limits, size limits, or possession limits exist for opossums.

Coyotes and Bobcats

Coyotes are considered varmints because they kill livestock and young wildlife. In addition, they kill many pet dogs and cats in suburban and rural areas. A population of coyotes can increase rapidly in an area.

When this happens, the animals become a nuisance to pet owners and area farmers and ranchers. Although the coyote has been intensively harvested in parts of the United States, its population has tended to increase across the country. Many states have broad hunting seasons for this animal. Some may have no bag limits. The season for coyotes varies from state to state and can be during the summer, fall, or winter months.

The bobcat is one of three types of wildcat found in North America. It is the most common wildcat on the continent. Bobcats will kill and eat a variety of small animals and birds. Because this predator does not discriminate between wild animals and valuable farm animals, it can be a nuisance to farmers and ranchers. The season for bobcats is usually during the fall and winter. States vary, but tend to set the season with snowy months to allow hunters to track these animals.

Bobcats are nocturnal animals. These powerful and swift hunters can pounce up to ten feet (three meters) when hunting prey. They can easily catch and eat a farmer's small livestock.

Prairie Dogs

Several types of prairie dog are found throughout the prairie and flat grassland areas of the western United States. These wild rodents live in large groups called villages. Sometimes five hundred or more prairie dogs live in one small area, in homes that they make by burrowing deep

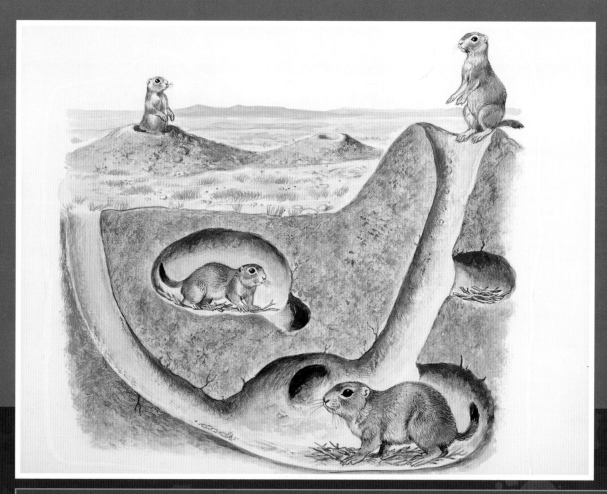

Prairie dogs live in underground burrows with many tunnels and chambers. Burrows have defined areas, such as nurseries and sleeping quarters. The small animals spend a lot of time making their burrows.

into the ground. If the villages are in a farmer's or rancher's pasture, the prairie dogs are considered a nuisance. They can eat and destroy farm crops and create deep-ground burrows into which livestock can trip, fall, and break a leg. In addition, large prairie dog populations are hosts to fleas and viruses that can cause plague or flea reactions in livestock or pets.

Hunters and Ethics

Hunters show good ethics when they are respectful of other people and their land. They must not trespass or hunt on private land without the permission of the landowner. It is also illegal to trespass. National and state forests are public lands that may require special permits for access to hunt. It is important to read the federal and state regulations to determine how hunting access can be obtained. Public land is owned by all citizens. Some public lands are wildlife management refuges in which hunting is generally not allowed. Varmint hunters on public property have a duty to treat the land with care. Whether on private or public land, hunters should know how to avoid damaging prairies and other fragile environments. For example, they should drive vehicles without harming the land or water in the area. People should always clean up after they are done hunting. It is good manners to pick up other people's litter. Some people are afraid of weapons or are uncomfortable seeing harvested animals. Hunters should not openly display their guns or harvest. They should also properly dispose of any offal (organs) and spent carcasses (animal parts that are not used).

In some states, prairie dogs are considered a nuisance animal and can be harvested year-round on private land. The season in that same state, on public land, can vary. In South Dakota, for instance, prairie dogs cannot be hunted in the spring. The hunting of these animals is not permitted in some public lands in the state. Few hunters pursue prairie dogs because hunting them requires a lot of time, travel, and expense. People who hunt these small rodents enjoy the challenge of extremely long, difficult shooting at small, moving animals.

Responsibilities of Varmint Hunters

Varmint hunters must know the hunting laws for the state. The laws include bag limits, legal hours, license requirements, seasons, any special regulations, and allowable gear such as headlights. Some states, for example, require a night permit to hunt. Hunters are responsible for knowing the type of firearms and archery equipment and when—the time of day or night—they can be used. People can get free hunting law booklets from local hunting license dealers, the state's department of natural of resources, or the department's Web site.

Shooting animals other than during a specified time of day or season is called poaching. It is illegal to poach, meaning it is a crime. When they are caught, poachers can receive legal penalties, including time in jail and large fines. Their guns and archery equipment will be taken away. They also may lose any vehicles that were used in the illegal hunt.

Every varmint hunter is responsible for making each hunt as safe as possible. Hunters must know how their rifles and other equipment work and how to shoot their firearms and archery safely around other hunters, animals, and on private or public property. Sometimes other people, such as wild berry pickers, campers, or hikers, may be using the land at the same time as a varmint hunter.

Minnesota Department of Natural Resources

MDNR#: 610-433-419

WILL E WALLEYE

123 BIG REEF
MINNESOTA LAKES, MN 12345

10

DOB: 06/01/1978
Drivers License: Q534666878963
Firearm Safety:

Height: 6'0
Weight: 200LBS
Gender: MALE
Eyes: GREEN

Expires February 28, 2011 (unless noted elsewhere)

211 - Resident Small GAme	$20.00
227 - HIP CERTIFICATION	$0.00

Total: $20.00

This license is NON-REFUNDABLE.

Licensee Signature: _____
I certify that I meet the citizenship requirements and have maintained a
legal residence in the state for a period of 60 days immediately preceding
the date of this application. My DNR license(s) are not otherwise revoked.

A small game hunting or a predator varmint license is required in many states that allow hunters to harvest varmint animals. States may have other requirements for nonresidents, such as paying an additional fee.

The flexibility for hunters to shoot at small, fast, and hard-to-hit wild animals during many months of the year provides excellent shooting practice for the hunter. Varmint hunting often requires long-distance shooting, sometimes a quarter mile (402 meters) or more. Many free resources on varmint hunting are available at public libraries, including books, magazines, and educational videos. Local shotgun or rifle clubs, gun dealers, and sporting clubs have experienced varmint hunters who are willing to teach beginning shooters. Wildlife managers, or biologists, with the state's department of natural resources and farm or ranch organizations can often provide advice and information for locating nuisance or overpopulated animals to hunt.

CHAPTER 2

VARMINT IDENTIFICATION AND BEHAVIOR

To be successful, hunters need to learn how to correctly identify the varmints they plan to hunt. They also must learn the habitat and behavior of the animals. Habits, which are predictable animal behaviors, include eating, sleeping, breeding, ways of communicating, and reacting to threats or attacks by predators. All animals have a home range in which they sleep, find food, mate, and raise offspring.

Raccoons

Raccoons have a ringed, bushy tail and a band of black fur around the eyes. The black fur looks like a mask. Its long fur is typically gray. Raccoons measure 24 to 42 inches (61 to 107 centimeters) in length, including their tail. Most weigh 8 to 20 pounds (3.6 to 9 kilograms). Raccoons are

If the local raccoon population becomes too large, the varmints will aggressively find and eat human garbage. Raccoons will sometimes dunk their food into water before eating it.

found throughout most of the United States and southern Canada. They prefer streams, rivers, lakes, woods, and swamps, but have adapted to other environments.

One reason raccoons are so widely found is that their fast, nimble front paws grab and handle all kinds of food. For instance, they pluck frogs, crayfish, clams, fish, and snails out of water. Another reason they are adaptable is that they eat nearly anything. In addition to water creatures, raccoons feed on slugs, insects, carrion (rotting, dead

Opossums are excellent tree climbers because of their sharp claws, which dig into bark. They also have a long, gripping tail that can be used as an extra limb.

animals), vegetables, fruits, nuts, and seeds. Sometimes they hunt young mice, rats, squirrels, and gophers. They will even open people's garbage cans and eat the garbage.

Raccoons live both on the ground and in trees. Nocturnal animals, they hunt for food at night and sleep and raise their young in dens during the day. Den sites include abandoned burrows, openings in rock piles, deserted buildings, fallen trees, and tree holes. Raccoons move to different dens frequently, but randomly. They live alone or in small family groups. Their mating season is from January to June, peaking from March to April.

The intelligent raccoon is a fierce fighter when cornered. It has sharp hearing and eyesight. Excellent swimmers, raccoons are equally adept on land and can run up to fifteen miles (twenty-four kilometers) per hour.

Opossums

The opossum is the only marsupial (mammal with a pouch) native to North America. The female carries her babies inside her pouch for two months. The opossum lives in the eastern United States and as far west as Texas. Populations are also along the West Coast. Hunters often find them in wet areas, especially streams and swamps.

How Opossums Get Away from Enemies

When threatened, an opossum might climb a tree to get away. It will growl, hiss, and bare its fifty razor-sharp teeth to scare off a predator. Otherwise it works its jaw so that drool drips out of its mouth and bubbles come out of its nose. Then the predator will think the opossum is sick and will not try to catch it to eat it. If escape is impossible and the animal becomes very stressed, it goes into shock and looks as though it has died from an illness. The opossum falls on its side, curls its body, opens its mouth, sticks out its tongue, and goes limp. It drools and poops smelly, green diarrhea. The predator leaves the opossum alone and goes away. When the opossum thinks the danger has passed, it wiggles its ears to listen and raises its head to look around. If the environment is safe, it leaves. If danger remains, it plays dead again.

Opossums are solitary and nocturnal. They eat most kinds of plants, including grass, nuts, and fruit. They also hunt for mice, insects, worms, snakes, birds, and eggs. In just minutes, one opossum can destroy a nest of game birds such as quail or break into a chicken coop and devour eggs. Sometimes opossums raid garbage cans and dumpsters.

Opossums nest in tree holes or in dens made by other animals. Their sharp claws and long, gripping tail help them climb trees swiftly. About the size of a pet cat, they measure 2.5 feet (76 cm) from nose to tail and weigh 9 to 13 pounds (4 to 6 kg). They have grayish-white fur, a long snout (nose, mouth, and jaw), pink nose, dark eyes, and large ears. Opossums usually mate from January through July.

Coyotes are difficult to hunt due to their keen vision, excellent sense of smell, and intelligence. They form packs for more effective hunting in the fall and winter.

Coyotes

Coyotes, also called brush wolves, will eat nearly anything, including insects, crops such as corn, and fruit. They hunt at night and most often prey on small animals such as mice, voles, and squirrels. They devour other animals such as fish and frogs. Sometimes they kill goats, calves, lambs, fawns, and pet cats and dogs. When they are unable to find fresh food, coyotes eat carrion. They typically stay away from people.

Along with its wide-ranging diet, the coyote can adapt to a variety of environments. It inhabits much of North America and continues to extend its range. To the west of the Mississippi River, the western coyote roams the open prairies, mountains, deserts, and some waterways. On the eastern side of the river, the habitat of the coyote is hardwood forests, brushy areas, and farmland.

Nimble and quick, coyotes can run up to forty miles (sixty-four km) per hour, but usually average twenty-five to thirty miles (forty to fifty km) per hour. They are highly intelligent and have excellent senses of vision and smell. These private, sneaky animals can move around without being seen or heard. Coyotes have pointed ears, a narrow muzzle (mouth, nose, and jaw), and grayish-brown fur with white chest hair. They measure about 48 inches (1.2 m) in length, including their 11- to 16-inch (28- to 41-cm) tail. They stand about 24 inches (0.6 m) high and weigh 25 to 50 pounds (9 to 23 kg).

Coyotes mate from January through March. Most live alone or in pairs. They may form packs of three or more to help hunt for food in the fall or winter. They communicate by howls, yips, yelps, and whines.

Bobcats

Bobcats are North America's most common wildcat. They can survive in a variety of habitats, except in areas of extreme cold, because they have

Bobcats are fierce hunters and can kill prey much bigger than themselves. They live about twelve to thirteen years in the wild. Although they are good swimmers, they seldom go into water.

soft pads instead of fur on the bottoms of their paws. They are found from southern Canada to Mexico and live in deserts, forests, mountains, or swamps. In the Southwest, bobcats prefer brushy areas, canyons, and wooded mesas (broad, flat-topped hills with one or more clifflike sides). Most people never see bobcats in the wild because they avoid people.

These wildcats have keen senses of vision and hearing. Often they quietly and slowly sneak up on their prey and catch it. They can leap and pounce up to ten feet (three m) on an animal, killing their meal immediately. Bobcats hunt for food at twilight and throughout the night. They eat mostly rabbits, but also feed on rodents, squirrels, porcupines, and sometimes young deer. They go after game birds such as wild turkeys, quails, pheasants, waterfowl, and farm chickens and geese. Usually bobcats look for prey on the ground, although they sometimes hunt while climbing in trees.

The bobcat has a short, black-tipped tail of four to seven inches (ten to eighteen cm) long. The head and body of an adult bobcat usually measures 26 to 41 inches (66 to 104 cm) long. Males weigh twenty to thirty pounds (nine to fourteen kg). Females are smaller, weighing eleven to twenty pounds (five to nine kg). The bobcat's fur is brown or brownish red with a white underbelly.

Bobcats are solitary. They mate in late winter or early spring. To raise their young, females make and live in dens under logs, in thickets, or in hollow trees.

Prairie Dogs

Prairie dogs are social, burrowing rodents that live on the prairies and open grasslands of the western United States. These plump animals have light brown fur, a short tail and legs, small ears, and sharp front claws that they use to dig tunnels. About the size of a football, an adult measures 9 to 15 inches (23 to 38 cm) long, including the tail, and weigh 1 to 3 pounds (0.5 to 1.4 kg). They have keen eyesight and a distinct, vocal communication system.

Five types of prairie dogs live in the United States. The most common types are the black-footed and the white-footed prairie dog. Prairie dogs live in large, tightly knit groups called towns or villages. They burrow deep into the ground to make rooms connected by tunnels of up to fifty feet (fifteen m) long. The tunnel entrances are ringed by a pile of soil. A town may contain hundreds of prairie dogs and typically covers less than half a square mile (1.3 km). If towns are in a farmer's or rancher's pasture, the prairie dogs eat the grasses that cattle and horses eat, leaving less food for livestock. They may also ruin hay, wheat, alfalfa, or corn crops.

Prairie dogs sleep at night. During the day, they feed on grasses, roots, and seeds. To warn of predators, some stand guard on the mounds at tunnel entrances. When predators approach, the guards give warning barks or yips and bob up and down, then call again. The guards and animals that are above ground then rush into the burrows. Prairie dogs can run up to thirty-five miles (sixty km) per hour for short distances. When danger has passed, the guards sound an all clear call.

During the winter, prairie dogs stay underground and hibernate (they are dormant, or inactive, during cold months). Black-footed prairie dogs mate in late January. The mating season for the white-footed prairie dogs is from March to April.

To learn more about raccoons, opossums, coyotes, bobcats, or prairie dogs, hunters can visit zoos, read books, and watch videos. Experienced wildlife managers, hunters, local farmers, and ranchers are other good resources for researching these animals. In addition, hunters may want to watch and photograph the animals in the wild before hunting them.

CHAPTER 3

PREPARING FOR THE HUNT

A successful varmint hunt requires preparation in many areas. Hunters will be matching their skills and wits against wild animals that are well adapted to survival. Many varmint predators have keen vision and hearing, and some have a strong sense of smell. Their swift movement far exceeds the human hunter. If they are not well prepared, hunters will probably not harvest their target and may not even see one.

Regulations, Licenses or Permits, and More

The most important prerequisite for varmint hunting is to obtain and read the state and federal regulations that control the hunt. Hunters must know what gun or archery equipment can be used on specific types of wild animals. They must know where, what days, what time of the day, and

All states have enforcement officers. They are also called game wardens or conservation officers. Their job is to help hunters and ensure that they are following regulations.

what hunting methods are allowed in their state and region. Hunting methods include the use of dogs or hunting at night. For instance, the prairie dog in most states is considered a nuisance and can be harvested year-round using any method. In contrast, the regulations for hunting bobcats in the neighboring states of Minnesota and Wisconsin are quite different. Local state departments of natural resources publish a hunting license book every year. This information is also found on these departments' Web sites.

Before going hunting, hunters must buy the proper licenses or permits. Every state offers beginning and adult hunter education programs. A hunter's successful completion of this course leads to a certificate of graduation. The age when young hunters can begin to hunt alone often depends on when they have earned their safety certificate.

In addition to state training programs, hunters can gain valuable knowledge about varmints, predators, and hunting from gun clubs, sporting clubs, and farm and ranch organizations such as 4-H and Future Farmers of America. Local hunters who are experienced with varmint hunting are often available to help beginning hunters. Rifle, shotgun, and archery clubs are common throughout the United States and Canada. They provide access to hunting preparation information, tips, and methods.

Accessing Private Land and Scouting

Gaining access to the particular varmint is important. It is critical that the varmint habitat is known and access to hunt that varmint is attained well in advance of the actual hunt. People use country maps, which identify land ownership, and topographic and aerial maps. All of these maps are usually available for free on the Web. Local state departments of natural resources, farm and ranch organizations, and local sporting clubs can lead beginning hunters to geographic areas, then to specific land parcels where varmint populations exist. Farmers and ranchers are usually enthusiastic about having hunters reduce a varmint population on their property.

Varmint hunting is often a way to reduce or control a nuisance animal population in a specific area. Every state has professional wildlife managers who can direct varmint hunters to the targeted animal's range. When an area has been determined to have a potentially high

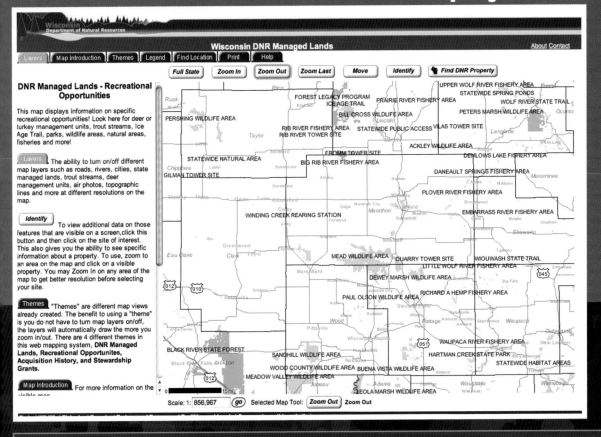

This map shows public land that is available for hunting. Hunters also find aerial, topographical, and land ownership maps helpful. Many of these maps are available free on county and state Web sites such as Wisconsin's Department of Natural Resources (http://dnrmaps.wisconsin.gov).

number of varmints, and the hunters have gained permission to hunt on private land, then scouting is a wise next step when preparing to hunt. Scouting to determine the best place to hunt is as important as the actual hunt. When scouting, hunters spend time walking, looking, and judging the land. They walk the property by daylight, taking note of bush areas or clearings and dangerous areas like cliffs, ditches, and rivers. They also look for physical landmarks so that they know which way to return when they are finished.

Using Camouflage When Hunting

Because varmints have excellent vision, hunters wear clothing that blends into whatever color the land and plants are at the location and season of the hunt. Camouflage clothing might be all white in snow, patchy green in dark green tree foliage, or dusky tan on open grasslands and prairies. Camouflage clothing includes gloves, hats, jackets, pants, and boots. Varmint hunters who are after predators like the coyote and bobcat may use face paint or a head-net because these animals need to be called in close for the harvest. Many shooters cover the shiny parts on their guns, scopes, and bow with camouflage tape or dull spray paint. Raccoons and coyotes have excellent hearing. When hunting these varmints, hunters find that wearing clothing made from quiet material is important. Popular choices of materials are polar fleece, wool, a well-washed polyester-cotton blend, or other fabric that has a low nap (a soft or fuzzy surface).

Digital and automatic still cameras and camcorders (video cameras) are common tools when scouting a region because they photograph the animals living there. While walking, a global positioning system (GPS) can be used to clearly and accurately mark future hunting sites on a map. Writing notes in a journal that is dedicated to future varmint hunting sites is another technique that can enhance successful hunts.

Learning the Skill of Sharp Shooting

Savvy varmint hunters select small-caliber, fast-speed, and low-trajectory (flight path) ammunition. However, the .22 long rifle caliber,

The ability to place a small bullet accurately on a target at long range requires much practice. The young woman wearing a cap is using a shooting bench to sight in her rifle.

20-gauge shotgun, or 30-pound bow is adequate to hunt raccoons, opossums, or bobcats. Larger weight and faster bullets, such as the .243 or 6mm Remington, are required to harvest large predators such as the coyote or long-range varmints like the prairie dog. The key for success with any rifle, gun, or bow is sharp shooting, or the ability to hit a small target. Sharp shooting is a skill that demands many hours of patient, concentrated practice. Hunters must know exactly how their gun operates, fires, and feels before shooting at a varmint.

The skill to shoot straight develops over time by taking hundreds or thousands of practice shots. Shooting from a solid rest or bench at a stationary target at different distances will greatly improve a hunter's ability to harvest varmints. Shooters should practice with targets on private land or public or private shooting ranges. In many areas, shooting ranges that charge a fee are available for practice.

Clothing and Other Gear

After scouting, a varmint hunter needs clothing that is matched to the hunting area. If swampy soil or mountainous or hilly land is the hunting site, hunters should have sturdy leather and rubber boots. Rain gear and waders may be necessary, too. Warm clothing is a must when hunters plan to sit for hours in the cold or snow. A camouflage parka with a flap-up hood is excellent outerwear when the hunt is predicted for cold areas or locations with strong winds.

Varmint hunters must be properly equipped for their personal safety and the safety of their dogs, particularly when they are hunting at night. Good hunting lights and extra batteries are essential for hunters to find their way through woods. Some hunting lights, such as for raccoons, fit onto special hardhats. The battery cable runs down one side of the hat to the waist and attaches to a battery pack that is placed in a pocket. Hunters adjust the brightness of the beam with a control knob.

Successful coyote hunters often wear camouflage clothing to blend into the background because of the varmint's sharp vision. Long-distance shooting requires a shooting stick tripod and scoped rifles.

Night hunters can also use baseball-type fabric caps that are fitted with mounting brackets on the visor to hold headlights. Hunters can choose belt clips for their lights or use headband headlights. Some raccoon hunters fit amber or red plastic lenses over their hunting lights. Animals notice the colored light less than a white light.

Hunters may use dogs when they are hunting some varmints. If they do so, they need to keep track of them as they chase through the woods after varmints. Dog collars equipped with lights are a good idea to use. Many hunters have tracking devices on their dogs' collars that help them find lost or injured dogs. Varmints typically run swiftly when chased by dogs. The varmint and chasing dogs may travel so quickly that hunters lose track of all the animals. A tracking device helps hunters find their dogs. Practicing with dogs at night before going on an actual hunt leads to hunting success and reduces the chance of the loss of a dog.

CHAPTER 4

How to Hunt

Each varmint is a small, quick-witted animal that lives in different habitats, such as grass prairie, desert, heavily wooded forests, or rocky hillsides. Each varmint also has different habits. In order to be successful, hunters must learn and apply different strategies for successfully hunting these animals.

Raccoons and Opossums

Raccoons and opossums are active at night, making it difficult or impossible to hunt them during the day. The method that consistently results in a good harvest is hunting with coon dogs. Dog breeds that hunt by scent include the Walker, bluetick, redtick, redbone, black-and-tan, and English coon dog. These dogs track and follow fresh varmint scents.

Hunting dogs with an excellent sense of smell are often used to hunt varmints at night. This bluetick coonhound has forced a bobcat into a tree, where hunters can harvest the varmint.

Raccoon and opossum hunting are usually done in small groups. The chase begins when two to four hunters release several coon dogs on a spoor, or fresh track. Because the tracking is done at night, hunters need to be aware of the land, water, and other road and area characteristics. The coon dogs chase and follow the fresh scent of a raccoon or opossum until the animal climbs a tree. The dogs circle the tree and continue to bark wildly. Meanwhile, the hunters follow the sound of the barking dogs.

Once at the site, hunters shoot the treed animal at close range, usually with a small-caliber rifle such as the .22 long rifle hollow point. Night hunters carry their rifles cased during the hunt and uncase them for the actual shots to harvest the raccoon or opossum. For safety, one hunter is designated as the shooter. Loaded guns at night are dangerous because it is difficult to know exactly where the muzzle is aimed. Shotguns can be used. However, at close range, the valuable hide and meat are ruined. Some hunters prefer archery equipment. They need to be careful while they are tracking and running through the woods because the bow and arrows could break as they hit unseen trees in the black of night.

Many night varmint hunters use a GPS tracking device to determine their exact location. Strong headlamps or flashlights are necessary for hunters to safely walk through the woods and see while shooting a treed varmint. Wise hunters always carry spare batteries.

Coyotes

Hunters usually go with three methods when hunting coyotes. One is to call coyotes to the hunter by making the sound of a wounded rabbit. Another technique is to bring the animals to a hunter by baiting them with meat. Hunters can also stalk this varmint on foot.

This hunter is using a coyote call that makes the sound of a dying rabbit. The varmint will respond to the call by walking into close shooting range.

Calling a coyote with a mouth-blown commercial call or an electronic player is effective during all months of the year. The call imitates the cry of a wounded or dying rabbit, the favorite food of coyotes. Although used any time of the day, calling works best at sunrise or sunset when coyotes are actively hunting. Before calling, hunters conceal themselves in blinds, or they wear camouflage clothing and remain still. They must be ready to make a fast shot at a swift target because coyotes within the hearing area approach the calling position quickly. To start, professionals recommend sitting quietly for ten to fifteen minutes, then calling loudly. Slowly tapering off the dying rabbit sound makes the call more realistic. Calling is louder as the night goes on to bring coyotes in from farther away. If no coyotes appear within an hour, the hunter moves to another location.

Coyote baiting is a customary hunting method. Hunters place bait (food) regularly in an area known to host a coyote population. The bait often is a dead deer or other roadkill animals. The local game warden may need to issue a permit for possession of a road-killed carcass (dead animal). Other bait includes offal (guts) from local farmers or ranchers or scraps of meat purchased from grocery or meat stores. The meat attracts birds of prey, such as eagles, magpies, crows, and vultures. In turn, the noisy calling of these birds attracts coyotes.

To bait effectively, hunters must be scent-free and wear clean clothes. They should hide within camouflage, such as a pit dug into the ground, a tree stand, or a ground blind. Hiding inside a brush pile also works well. Shots at feeding coyotes are usually taken at long range. Hunters use fast-velocity, low-trajectory (flight path), small-grain caliber rifles like the .22/250 or .25/06 Remington. When hunting varmints, serious big game hunters often use large-caliber rifles, such as .270 or .30-06, loaded with lightweight bullets. Hunters can set up automatic, digital, or video cameras to scout the time of day and number of feeding coyotes.

Covering the Hunter's Scent

Hunters need to make sure that coyotes cannot smell them. Coyotes are wild members of the dog family. All dogs have a keen sense of smell and can easily detect a human in their area. Any human or unusual scent alerts the coyote to an intruder. Hunters must control odor from perspiration, urination, and so on. Sometimes hunters must relieve themselves in the woods. They should dig a hole, relieve themselves, and then bury their waste and any used toilet paper. Afterward, hunters should wash their hands before handling their gun. Human odor is minimized by hunting downwind of coyotes and keeping all clothing clean and free of human scent. Using soap and laundry detergent without a scent is recommended for washing clothing. Sporting goods stores sell scent-free laundry soaps. Hunting equipment should not smell like cleaning oil and cleaning solvents during the actual hunt.

The third strategy to harvest coyotes requires snow. Two or more hunters drive along on country roads in the winter and look for fresh coyote tracks. Once fresh spoor is located, one hunter is stationed in an area ahead of the coyote's direction of travel. The other hunter returns to the fresh tracks and slowly walks or stalks the coyote. This hunting style requires good binoculars to scan the area ahead for signs of the coyote. If successful, the tracking hunter flushes the coyote past the second posted hunter. Otherwise, the tracker might sneak up on a feeding or sleeping coyote. Wind direction is important because a coyote's sense of smell is very good. Hunters use a compass or GPS to know their position. Cell phones are useful, where legal, for the team of hunters to communicate a coyote's unpredictable escape path during the hunt.

Bobcats

Bobcat hunting methods depend on the hunting area and time of year. The most common and successful strategy for hunting the bobcat is by calling. Like coyotes, bobcats are called by the sound of a dying or wounded rabbit. The shrill, wailing sound carries long distances, and a bobcat within hearing distance moves into the area. The call imitates

Successful bobcat and coyote hunters use game or predator calls, a proper scoped rifle, and camouflage clothing. A game call is a mouth-blown or electronic call that makes sounds that appeal to the varmint.

the distress and dying sound of a rabbit, which is easy prey for a bobcat. Hunters can make this presentation even more attractive by hanging a thin, dark strip of cloth or a dark feather from a low branch. The moving cloth or feather draws the bobcat's attention in the snowy white background and away from the hunter.

To harvest, hunters use a small-caliber rifle identical to the one used for coyote hunting. Nonexpanding bullets are critical so as not to damage the pelt (fur). During calling, bobcat hunters should wear full camouflage, such as all-white clothing in the winter with snow or regular camouflage clothing when no snow is present. They must remain quiet and motionless until the animal comes within shooting range.

In some states, bobcat hunting with dogs, such as foxhounds, is permissible. Using dogs requires the hunters to find bobcat tracks that are crossing a road or trail and then releasing the hounds to follow the fresh spoor. Eventually, the wildcat tires and climbs a tree or turns to fight the dogs while it is at bay. The hunters follow behind the howling dogs and harvest the bobcat. While the bobcat is treed, the shot is at close range, so hunters use small-caliber rifles or archery.

Prairie Dogs

To hunt prairie dogs, hunters must find a village of animals on an accessible prairie. Many ranchers seek out and appreciate shooters who will reduce or eliminate a local population. Active during the day, prairie dogs quickly retreat to their underground burrows when they are threatened. Hunters need to be concerned about the animal's excellent vision. This characteristic can be overcome by long-distance shooting.

Typically, hunters set up firm benches or tripods for stability, which allow accurate shooting up to 200 to 300 yards (183 to 274 m) at these small targets. They need a clear line of sight and a sturdy backstop, such as a hill, in the direction they will be shooting. Small-grain, fast-caliber

Prairie dog hunting can require shooting up to 300 yards (274 m) or more. A shooting bipod or tripod and scoped gun are required for accurate bullet placement.

rifles with scopes are used because of the long distance of the targets. Scope magnification is typically 5x10 power. Some varmint hunters prefer 20 power.

Most serious prairie dog shooters use a high-magnification scope on a tripod to visually scan the prairie. When prairie dogs are located, the shooters switch to rifles. Two or three rifles per hunter are needed because the fast, constant shooting makes the rifle barrel red-hot and destroys the accuracy. Other essential equipment to hunt prairie dogs includes good binoculars, shaded shooting glasses, and a brimmed hat.

CHAPTER 5

STEPS TO TAKE AFTER A HARVEST

The distinction of an accomplished varmint hunter is how they carry out their post-hunt activities. After a harvest, hunters must immediately care for the meat and hide. They need to check their hunting equipment for repairs and store it safely. They also should note accurate and important information about the hunt to help guarantee success in the future.

Using the Meat

A varmint requires attention immediately after the harvest. To make certain the meat is tasty and safe, hunters must cool the carcass as soon as possible. If the weather is forty degrees Fahrenheit (four degrees Celsius) or below, taking the internal organs from the body cavity allows the carcass to cool quickly. If the hunting is done during warm weather, gutting the animal and putting the carcass on ice or in a cooler as soon as practical is mandatory for obtaining quality meat and hides.

Raccoon, opossum, and prairie dogs have edible, savory meat if cooled quickly. The meat needs to be butchered and sliced into small portions and cleaned in cold water. The meat is then ready for cooking. For future use, the meat is packaged, labeled, and frozen.

Meat that is cooled quickly, cleaned, and properly cared for is a source of pride for many hunters. Good hunters often share their rewards with family and friends. A variety of resources, including books, magazines, and Web sites, are devoted to wild game meat, including the butchering, care, and preparation of the animals for eating. People enjoy raccoon and opossum meat in stews, chilies, and soups. They can slow cook, grill, fry, barbecue, roast, or even smoke the meat for a delicious meal.

Removing Hides

The raccoon, coyote, and bobcat are valuable furbearers. When properly cared for, their plush, thick hide is valuable for clothing. People who live in northern latitudes, like Alaska, Canada, Russia, and northern China, use wild animal hides to make warm winter clothing.

Hunters must care for the fur of their harvested animal to ensure that it is usable. They must pay special attention so as not to damage the hair because of rough handling, such as pulling the animal through brush, swamps, or grass. Many varmint hunters strip or skin the hide from the carcass while they are still in the woods. They can then place several hides into a packsack for carrying through the woods. Because people do not eat coyote and bobcat meat, skinning the collected animals in the woods and leaving the carcass for other predators to eat

People who live in northern climates, such as this woman in Moscow, Russia, who is wearing a raccoon coat, appreciate the warmth of natural animal fur for their winter clothing. The fur of bobcats and coyotes is also used to make warm clothing.

solves two problems at once. The valuable fur hide is protected from hair damage, and the carcass and offal provide an easy meal for other wildlife. Birds and wild mammals of all types feed heavily on carcass meat and bones left to rot in the woods after harvests. Eagles, buzzards, and crows feast on carrion, and small rodents chew up the bones for calcium, a necessary nutrient for bones and teeth.

Removing the hide of all varmints is accomplished by using the same basic method. Hunters hang the animal by both hind legs and cut the hide completely around each hind foot. They make an incision (cut) on the underside of each leg down from the foot to the vent (anus). Then they pull the hide down and off the carcass, similar to pulling off a glove. Next, hunters carefully cut around the ears, eyes, and nose, and pull the hide completely free of the carcass. A small, sharp knife is the only tool required to skin a hide. Books and videos are available that show the hide removal and meat butchering methods used for varmints.

If hunters do not want to prepare their hides, they can take their animals to professional fur buyers who will skin the hides and purchase them from the hunters. Fur buyers can be found throughout the United States. This transaction is common with coyotes, raccoons, and bobcats. Opossum and prairie dog hides are not commercially used. Hunters discard these hides with the offal and carcass.

Most varmint hunters seek their targeted wild animals on private land. It is essential—and common courtesy—that hunters thank the landowner after a hunt. Private land owners always enjoy some gesture of appreciation, such as an offering of meat, a thank-you card, or volunteer work on their property or with their livestock. The next hunt totally depends on access to the land on which the varmint lives. Experienced hunters do not take for granted permission to access private land. In addition to helping ranchers and farmers control nuisance pests, many varmint hunters and landowners become long-term friends.

Documenting the Hunt

Varmint hunting is enhanced in both successful harvests and enjoyable memories by documenting the hunt. Digital photographs and videos of the wild animals and the hunt give much satisfaction and pleasure during the off-season. Hunters should write a journal entry after every hunt. Journaling can be done on paper or electronically. Capturing the essentials of who, what, when, where, and how from each outdoor attempt to hunt varmints provides a basis for future hunts. The temperature, wind direction, and storm fronts should also be documented

After a hunt, wise hunters document where they hunted, what happened, and what they can do better in the next hunt. These hunters are reviewing a ranch map after hunting coyotes.

along with details of the hunt. The journal should include maps of the area that was hunted. Most state departments of natural resources provide free topographical maps. Aerial maps are free on Web sites such as Google Earth (http://earth.google.com).

Successful varmint harvests are based on the skill, ability, and experience of a hunter. This requires memory of precise details of the hunt that allowed success or resulted in failure. The time spent hunting varmints is usually limited by other important activities such as school, family, friends, work, or other obligations. When the opportunity to hunt arises, having details of previous outdoor varmint shooting experiences gives hunters a better chance to score a hit on the targeted varmint.

Technology for the Hunt

Various technologies give hunters an easy, quick, and reliable way to make advanced preparations based on the details of past hunts. Some digital cameras have GPS devices as part of the memory so that when a photo is taken, the exact location (latitude and longitude) is printed on the photo. This location can be downloaded onto topographical or aerial maps when the hunter has returned home. It is easy for the varmint hunter to keep maps at home or carry them into the woods with locations marked for placing blinds, calling in varmints, locating prairie dog villages, or identifying dangerous landforms such as cliffs with steep drop-offs. The locations of varmint dens, feeding areas, or regularly followed game trails can be mapped and plotted on topographic or aerial maps. Whether using a handheld GPS, a camera with built-in GPS, or memory, the marking of maps helps the hunter efficiently select excellent scoping, calling, or hunting sites for future hunts.

Caring for Equipment

Once the meat and hide are cared for, savvy hunters focus on the equipment and clothing that were used in the hunt. This step should be done whether or not the hunt was successful. Hunters dry, clean, and oil their guns, scopes, and archery equipment. They look for any breaks or damaged parts that need repair. Because prairie dog shooters may have fired hundreds of rounds of ammunition, they need to give their rifle bore special attention. Rifle shooters thoroughly scrub the barrel's bore with solvent and brass brushes until the copper and lead deposits

Cleaning guns properly is critical for the shooter's safety and for the next successful hunt. It is important to remove dirt and moisture that can pit or rust rifles.

are removed. Then applying a final light oil coating protects the steel bore from rusting. Hunters who clean and check their equipment are well prepared to hunt again. Experienced hunters have safe, dependable, and established areas in their garage or homes where all hunting equipment is stored for safety and fast retrieval when the next hunt comes up. Gun owners are strongly encouraged to store all rifles, shotguns, and pistols in a secure metal safe.

Varmint hunters often use some electronic equipment. They may have headlamps, flashlights, calling devices, GPS devices, range finders, pocket digital cameras, and camcorders. When hunting in groups, two-way radios are often used. Hunters need to remove the batteries from all electronic devices, then clean and store the equipment. Having an organized, efficient storage area for equipment allows hunters to spend time preparing and planning the next hunt instead of retrieving it at the last minute or trying to find clothing and equipment that they need.

Varmint hunting gives the hunter the pride of knowing that the landowner has benefited from the hunt by reducing or eliminating a pesky varmint population. The hunt also benefits the hunter in making friendships with landowners that may lead to private land access during future big or small game hunting.

GLOSSARY

ammunition Bullets and gun powder used in firearms.

archery The skill of shooting with a bow and arrow.

bag limit The number of a particular type of animal that a hunter can harvest during a day.

barrel The metal tube of a rifle.

blind A shelter, often camouflaged, used for concealing hunters.

bore The hollow part inside a gun barrel.

butcher To process an animal's meat into usable sizes.

caliber The inside diameter of the barrel of a rifle or the diameter of a bullet.

camouflage Anything that conceals people or equipment by making them appear to be part of the natural surroundings.

carrion Rotting, dead animals.

dress To prepare a recently harvested animal so that its body temperature lowers and the meat stays fresh.

flush To cause a hidden animal to suddenly move out of hiding.

furbearer An animal whose skin is covered with fur, especially fur that is commercially valuable.

game Wild animals hunted for food or sport.

global positioning system (GPS) A handheld computer that can calculate an exact position using a global positioning satellite.

habitat The area or environment where an animal lives.

harvest The act of shooting and recovering an animal.

illegal Against the law.

nocturnal Active at night.

poacher A person who takes game in a forbidden area or game that is illegal to take.

possession limit The maximum number of a type of animal that can be in a hunter's possession at any time.

predator An animal that eats another living animal.

prerequisite A thing that is required as a prior condition for something else to happen or exist.

prey An animal hunted or caught for food.

scope A small telescope on a rifle barrel.

season Length of time to hunt specific game.

spoor The track or trail of an animal, especially a wild animal.

target Something that is aimed at to shoot with firearms or bow and arrow.

trespass To unlawfully enter a person's property.

Canadian Parks and Wilderness Society

506–250 City Centre Avenue

Ottawa, ON K1R 6K7

Canada

(800) 333-9453

Web site: http://www.cpaws.org

This organization focuses on protecting many important areas of Canada's
wilderness.

Canadian Shooting Sports Association

7 Director Court, Unit #106

Vaughan, ON L4L 4S5

Canada

(888) 873-4339

Web site: http://www.cdnshootingsports.org

The Canadian Shooting Sports Association promotes shooting sports, including hunting and archery. It supports and sponsors competitions and youth
programs and conducts training classes.

International Hunter Education Association

2727 West 92nd Avenue, Suite 103

Federal Heights, CO 80260

(303) 430-7233

Web site: http://www.ihea.com

The International Hunter Education Association is the professional association
for state and provincial wildlife conservation agencies and the instructors
who teach hunter education in North America.

National Bowhunter Education Foundation

P.O. Box 180757

Fort Smith, AR 72918

(479) 649-9036

Web site: http://www.nbef.org

The foundation provides bowhunting education and classes across the
United States.

National Rifle Association of America

11250 Waples Mill Road

Fairfax, VA 22030

(800) 672-3888

Web site: http://www.nra.org

The National Rifle Association of America provides firearms education
throughout the world.

National Shooting Sports Foundation

Flintlock Ridge Office Center

11 Mile Hill Road

Newtown, CT 06470-2359

(203) 426-1320

Web site: http://www.nssf.org

The mission of the National Shooting Sports Foundation is to promote,
protect, and preserve hunting and the shooting sports.

National Wildlife Federation

11100 Wildlife Center Drive

Reston, VA 20190-5362

(800) 822-9919

Web site: http://www.nwf.org

The National Wildlife Federation works to protect and restore wildlife habitat.

U.S. Fish and Wildlife Service

1849 C Street NW

Washington, DC 20240

(800) 344-9453

Web site: http://www.fws.gov

This government agency is dedicated to the conservation, protection, and enhancement of wildlife and plants and their habitats. Its primary responsibility is management of these important natural resources for the American public.

U.S. Forest Service

Attn: Office of Communication

Mailstop: 1111

1400 Independence Avenue SW

Washington, DC 20250-1111

(800) 832-1355

Web site: http://www.fs.fed.us

An agency of the U.S. Department of Agriculture, the Forest Service manages the millions of acres of public lands in national forests and grasslands.

Web Sites

Due to the changing nature of Internet links, Rosen Publishing has developed an online list of Web sites related to the subject of this book. This site is updated regularly. Please use this link to access the list:

http://www.rosenlinks.com/hunt/varm

Andrews, Harris, and James A. Smith. *The Pocket Field Dressing Guide: The Complete Guide to Dressing Game*. Accokeek, MD: Stoeger Publishing Company, 2007.

Bechdel, Tom. *Coyote Hunting: The Eastern Coyote*. Terra Alta, WV: Headline Books, 2006.

Bynum, Bill. *Predator Hunting: A Complete Guide to Hunting Coyotes, Foxes, Bobcats, Bears, and More*. Guilford, CT: The Lyons Press, 2004.

Gross, W. H. *Young Beginner's Guide to Shooting & Archery: Tips for Gun and Bow*. Minnetonka, MN: Creative Publishing international, 2009.

Johnson, M. D. *Successful Small Game Hunting: Rediscovering Our Hunting Heritage*. Iola, WI: Krause Publications, 2003.

Lauber, Lon E. *Bowhunter's Guide to Accurate Shooting*. Minnetonka, MN: Creative Publishing international, 2005.

Lewand, Andrew L. *The Coyote Chronicles: Exciting Coyote Hunting Stories and Tips & Strategies for their Success!* Charleston, SC: CreateSpace, 2009.

Lewis, Gary. *Complete Guide to Hunting: Basic Techniques for Gun & Bow Hunters*. Minnetonka, MN: Creative Publishing international, 2008.

Schoby, Michael. *Successful Predator Hunting*. Iola, WI: Krause Publications, 2003.

Simmons, Nancy. *Exploring the World of Mammals*. New York City, NY: Chelsea House, 2007.

Spomer, Ron. *Predator Hunting: Proven Strategies That Work from East to West* (Outdoorsman's Edge). Upper Saddle River, NJ: Creative Homeowner, 2004.

Stilson, Glen. *Ready for Anything: A Guide to Predator Hunting*. Charleston, SC: CreateSpace, 2009.

Young, Jon, and Tiffany Morgan. *Animal Tracking Basics*. Harrisburg, PA: Stackpole Books, 2007.

BIBLIOGRAPHY

Blair, Gerry. *Predator Calling with Gerry Blair*. Iola, WI: Krause Publications, 2007.

Brakefield, Tom. *Small Game Hunting*. Philadelphia, PA: J. B. Lippincott Company, 1978.

Churchill, James. *Field Dressing Small Game and Fowl*. Harrisburg, PA: Stackpole Books, 1987.

Creative Publishing. *Dressing and Cooking Wild Game*. Chanhassen, MN: Creative Publishing, 2000.

Daniels, Martha. "Raccoon Hunting with Jake." The Missouri Conservationist for Kids Online, 2010. Retrieved March 10, 2010 (http://mdc.mo.gov/kids/out-in/2002/03/2.htm).

Geer, Galen. *Meat on the Table: Modern Small-Game Hunting*. Boulder, CO: Paladin Press, 1985.

GunnersDen. "Bobcat Hunting." 2010. Retrieved March 10, 2010 (http://www.gunnersden.com/index.htm.shooting-hunting-bobcat.html).

GunnersDen. "Coyote Hunting." 2010. Retrieved March 10, 2010 (http://www.gunnersden.com/index.htm.shooting-hunting-coyote.html).

GunnersDen. "Varmint/Predator Hunting." 2007. Retrieved March 10, 2010 (http://www.gunnersden.com/index.htm.hunting-varmint.html).

Harrington, Dan. (Avid Hunter, Rice Lake, WI). In discussion with the author, March 2010.

Kansas Department of Wildlife and Parks. "Virginia Opossum." 2010. Retrieved March 10, 2010 (http://www.kdwp.state.ks.us/news/Hunting/Furharvesting/Furbearers/Virginia-Opossum).

Lawrence, H. Lea. *The Ultimate Guide to Small Game and Varmint Hunting: How to Hunt Squirrels, Rabbits, Hares, Woodchucks, Coyotes, Foxes and More*. Guilford, CT: The Lyons Press, 2002.

Maas, David R. *North American Game Animals*. Minnetonka, MN: Cy Decosse, 1995.

National Shooting Sports Foundation. "The Ethical Hunter." Pamphlet, 2006.

Outdoor Empire Publishing. *Minnesota Firearms Safety Hunter Education, Student Manual*. Seattle, WA: Outdoor Empire Publishing, 2001.

Peterson, David H. (Hunter Education Instructor, Two Harbors, MN). In discussion with the author, March 2010.

Schneck, Marcus. *The North America Hunter's Handbook*. Philadelphia, PA: Running Press, 1991.

U.S. Geological Survey. "Small Mammals of North Dakota: Black-tailed Prairie Dog." Northern Prairie Wildlife Research Center, August 3, 2006. Retrieved March 10, 2010 (http://www.npwrc.usgs.gov/resource/mammals/mammals/prairie.htm).

Watson, Steve. (Avid Varmint Hunter, Cambridge, MN). In discussion with the author, March 2010.

About the Author

Judy Monroe Peterson is married to an avid hunter who has more than fifty years of hunting experience. She is a writer and editor of K–12 and post-high school curriculum materials.

About the Consultant

Benjamin Cowan has more than twenty years of big game and small game hunting experience. In addition to being an avid hunter, Cowan is also a member of many conservation organizations. He resides in west Tennessee.

Photo Credits

Cover, back cover (background), pp. 1, 3, 7 (left), 18 (right), 22 (background), 28 (right), 32 (background), 37 (right), 42 (background), 46 (right), 51 (background) © www.istockphoto.com/Nick Tzolov; book art (camouflage) © www.istockphoto.com/Dar Yang Yan; back cover (silhouette), chapter art (silhouette) Hemera/Thinkstock; chapter art (silhouette) © www.istockphoto.com/Michael Olson; p. 5 Steve Maslowski/Visuals Unlimited; pp. 8, 25, 48 Shutterstock; pp. 10–11, 16 State of Minnesota, Department of Natural Resources; p. 12 Joseph Van Os/Riser/Getty Images; p. 13 De Agostini Picture Library/De Agostini/Getty Images; p. 19 Michael Durham/Visuals Unlimited; pp. 20–21 Hemera Technologies/Photos.com/Thinkstock; p. 23 Jack Milchanowski/Visuals Unlimited/Getty Photos; p. 29 Georgia Department of Natural Resources, Wildlife Resources Division; p. 31 Wisconsin Department of Natural Resources; pp. 33, 35, 38, 43, 45, 50, 52 Judd Cooney; p. 40 Mike Mergen/Bloomberg via Getty Images.

Designer: Nicole Russo; Editor: Kathy Kuhtz Campbell;
Photo Researcher: Marty Levick